CU00869074

*In Celebration Of:*

................................................................

................................................................

# *Guests*

Name　　　　　　　　　　　　　　　　　　Thoughts and Memories

......................................................................

　　　　　　　　　　　　　　　　　　......................................................................

　　　　　　　　　　　　　　　　　　......................................................................

　　　　　　　　　　　　　　　　　　......................................................................

......................................................................

　　　　　　　　　　　　　　　　　　......................................................................

　　　　　　　　　　　　　　　　　　......................................................................

　　　　　　　　　　　　　　　　　　......................................................................

......................................................................

　　　　　　　　　　　　　　　　　　......................................................................

　　　　　　　　　　　　　　　　　　......................................................................

　　　　　　　　　　　　　　　　　　......................................................................

......................................................................

　　　　　　　　　　　　　　　　　　......................................................................

　　　　　　　　　　　　　　　　　　......................................................................

　　　　　　　　　　　　　　　　　　......................................................................

Name

## Guests

Thoughts and Memories

# *Guests*

Name

Thoughts and Memories

# *Guests*

Name                               Thoughts and Memories

Name  Thoughts and Memories

## Guests

Name

Thoughts and Memories

Name

*Guests*

Thoughts and Memories

## _Guests_

Name                                     Thoughts and Memories

Name  Thoughts and Memories

Name    *Guests*    Thoughts and Memories

Name     *Guests*     Thoughts and Memories

Name                    *Guests*                    Thoughts and Memories

........................................................    ........................................................

........................................................

........................................................

........................................................

........................................................    ........................................................

........................................................

........................................................

........................................................

........................................................    ........................................................

........................................................

........................................................

........................................................

........................................................    ........................................................

........................................................

........................................................

........................................................

Name  Thoughts and Memories

Name    *Guests*    Thoughts and Memories

# Guests

Name                          Thoughts and Memories

......................................................................          ......................................................................

......................................................................

......................................................................

......................................................................

......................................................................          ......................................................................

......................................................................

......................................................................

......................................................................

......................................................................          ......................................................................

......................................................................

......................................................................

......................................................................

......................................................................          ......................................................................

......................................................................

......................................................................

......................................................................

## Guests

Name

Thoughts and Memories

## Guests

Name

Thoughts and Memories

## *Guests*

Name

Thoughts and Memories

Name  Thoughts and Memories

Name  *Guests*  Thoughts and Memories

## Guests

Name

Thoughts and Memories

Name

*Guests*

Thoughts and Memories

## Guests

Name

Thoughts and Memories

........................................................

........................................................
........................................................
........................................................
........................................................

........................................................

........................................................
........................................................
........................................................
........................................................

........................................................

........................................................
........................................................
........................................................
........................................................

........................................................

........................................................
........................................................
........................................................
........................................................

## Guests

Name                              Thoughts and Memories

## *Guests*

Name

Thoughts and Memories

Name                    *Guests*                    Thoughts and Memories

Name

Thoughts and Memories

Name       *Guests*       Thoughts and Memories

..................................................................

..................................................................

..................................................................

..................................................................

..................................................................

..................................................................

..................................................................

..................................................................

..................................................................

..................................................................

..................................................................

..................................................................

..................................................................

..................................................................

..................................................................

..................................................................

..................................................................

..................................................................

..................................................................

Name

## Guests

Thoughts and Memories

## *Guests*

Name                    Thoughts and Memories

Name

## *Guests*

Thoughts and Memories

Name

*Guests*

Thoughts and Memories

## Guests

Name                                Thoughts and Memories

Name

# *Guests*

Thoughts and Memories

## Guests

Name

Thoughts and Memories

Name     *Guests*     Thoughts and Memories

Name
Guests
Thoughts and Memories

Name                    *Guests*                    Thoughts and Memories

## Guests

Name                    Thoughts and Memories

........................................    ........................................

........................................

........................................

........................................

........................................    ........................................

........................................

........................................

........................................

........................................    ........................................

........................................

........................................

........................................

........................................    ........................................

........................................

........................................

........................................

## *Guests*

Name                                    Thoughts and Memories

# *Guests*

Name                                    Thoughts and Memories

Name     *Guests*     Thoughts and Memories

Name

## Guests

Thoughts and Memories

Name

*Guests*

Thoughts and Memories

Name

*Guests*

Thoughts and Memories

## Guests

Name                             Thoughts and Memories

Name  Thoughts and Memories

Name

*Guests*

Thoughts and Memories

## *Guests*

Name                    Thoughts and Memories

Name    *Guests*    Thoughts and Memories

## Guests

Name                                    Thoughts and Memories

....................................    ....................................
                                        ....................................
                                        ....................................
                                        ....................................

....................................    ....................................
                                        ....................................
                                        ....................................
                                        ....................................

....................................    ....................................
                                        ....................................
                                        ....................................
                                        ....................................

....................................    ....................................
                                        ....................................
                                        ....................................
                                        ....................................

Name          *Guests*          Thoughts and Memories

Name

# *Guests*

Thoughts and Memories

Name                    *Guests*                    Thoughts and Memories

## Guests

Name          Thoughts and Memories

Name     *Guests*     Thoughts and Memories

Name

## Guests

Thoughts and Memories

Name

*Guests*

Thoughts and Memories

Name  Thoughts and Memories

Name

*Guests*

Thoughts and Memories

Name

*Guests*

Thoughts and Memories

Name

# Guests

Thoughts and Memories

Name  Thoughts and Memories

Name                    *Guests*                    Thoughts and Memories

Name

*Guests*

Thoughts and Memories

Name

## Guests

Thoughts and Memories

Name  Thoughts and Memories

Name  *Guests*  Thoughts and Memories

Name  Thoughts and Memories

Name

*Guests*

Thoughts and Memories

Name

*Guests*

Thoughts and Memories

Name     *Guests*     Thoughts and Memories

......................................................     ......................................................

    ......................................................

    ......................................................

    ......................................................

......................................................     ......................................................

    ......................................................

    ......................................................

    ......................................................

......................................................     ......................................................

    ......................................................

    ......................................................

    ......................................................

......................................................     ......................................................

    ......................................................

    ......................................................

    ......................................................

Name *Guests* Thoughts and Memories

Name

# Guests

Thoughts and Memories

Name

*Guests*

Thoughts and Memories

Name      *Guests*      Thoughts and Memories

## Guests

Name

Thoughts and Memories

......................................................

......................................................
......................................................
......................................................
......................................................

......................................................

......................................................
......................................................
......................................................
......................................................

......................................................

......................................................
......................................................
......................................................
......................................................

......................................................

......................................................
......................................................
......................................................
......................................................

## *Guests*

Name                                    Thoughts and Memories

.................................................                  .................................................

.................................................                  .................................................

                                                                  .................................................

                                                                  .................................................

.................................................                  .................................................

                                                                  .................................................

                                                                  .................................................

                                                                  .................................................

.................................................                  .................................................

                                                                  .................................................

                                                                  .................................................

                                                                  .................................................

.................................................                  .................................................

                                                                  .................................................

                                                                  .................................................

                                                                  .................................................

Name

*Guests*

Thoughts and Memories

Name

*Guests*

Thoughts and Memories

# *Guests*

Name                    Thoughts and Memories

........................................    ........................................
                                            ........................................
                                            ........................................
                                            ........................................

........................................    ........................................
                                            ........................................
                                            ........................................
                                            ........................................

........................................    ........................................
                                            ........................................
                                            ........................................
                                            ........................................

........................................    ........................................
                                            ........................................
                                            ........................................
                                            ........................................

## Guests

Name

Thoughts and Memories

Name

## Guests

Thoughts and Memories

Name
## Guests
Thoughts and Memories

Name

## Guests

Thoughts and Memories

Name     *Guests*     Thoughts and Memories

Name  Thoughts and Memories

## Guests

Name

Thoughts and Memories

Name

## Guests

Thoughts and Memories

## *Guests*

Name

Thoughts and Memories

Name

*Guests*

Thoughts and Memories

Name  *Guests*  Thoughts and Memories

Name

*Guests*

Thoughts and Memories

## *Guests*

Name                     Thoughts and Memories

Name

# *Guests*

Thoughts and Memories

## Guests

Name                                    Thoughts and Memories

...........................................    ...........................................

...........................................    ...........................................

...........................................    ...........................................

...........................................    ...........................................

...........................................    ...........................................

...........................................    ...........................................

...........................................    ...........................................

...........................................    ...........................................

...........................................    ...........................................

...........................................    ...........................................

...........................................    ...........................................

...........................................    ...........................................

...........................................    ...........................................

...........................................    ...........................................

...........................................    ...........................................

...........................................    ...........................................

## Guests

Name

Thoughts and Memories

Name            *Guests*            Thoughts and Memories

Printed in Great Britain
by Amazon

75766757R00059